NEW ENGLAND PATRIOTS · SUPER BOWL CHAMPIONS

# XXXVI, FEBRUARY 3, 2002

## 20-17 VERSUS ST. LOUIS RAMS

# XXXVIII, FEBRUARY 1, 2004

## 32-29 VERSUS CAROLINA PANTHERS

# XXXIX, FEBRUARY 6, 2005

## 24-21 VERSUS PHILADELPHIA EAGLES

# SUPER BOWL CHAMPIONS

## NEW ENGLAND PATRIOTS

AARON FRISCH

CREATIVE EDUCATION

COVER: DEFENSIVE TACKLE RICHARD SEYMOUR

PAGE 2: KICKER ADAM VINATIERI CELEBRATING A
PATRIOTS WIN

RIGHT: LINEBACKER ADALIUS THOMAS MAKING A TACKLE

Published by Creative Education
P.O. Box 227, Mankato, Minnesota 56002
Creative Education is an imprint of The Creative Company
www.thecreativecompany.us

Book and cover design by Blue Design (www.bluedes.com)
Art direction by Rita Marshall
Printed by Corporate Graphics in the United States of
America

Photographs by Dreamstime (Rosco), Getty Images (Arthur
Anderson/NFL, Timothy A. Clary/AFP, David Drapkin, Steve
Dunwell, Gin Ellis/NFL Photos, Jeff Haynes/AFP, Walter Iooss
Jr./Sports Illustrated, Streeter Lecka, Andy Lyons, NFL,
Darryl Norenburg/NFL, Joe Robbins, Damian Strohmeyer/
Sports Illustrated)

Library of Congress Cataloging-in-Publication Data

Frisch, Aaron.
New England Patriots / by Aaron Frisch.
p. cm. — (Super Bowl champions)
Includes index.
Summary: An elementary look at the New England Patriots
professional football team, including its formation in 1960,
most memorable players, Super Bowl championships, and
stars of today.
ISBN 978-1-60818-022-6
1. New England Patriots (Football team)—History—Juvenile
literature. I. Title. II. Series.

GV956.N36F75 2011
796.332'64'0974461—dc21      2009053506

CPSIA: 040110 PO1141

First Edition
9 8 7 6 5 4 3 2 1

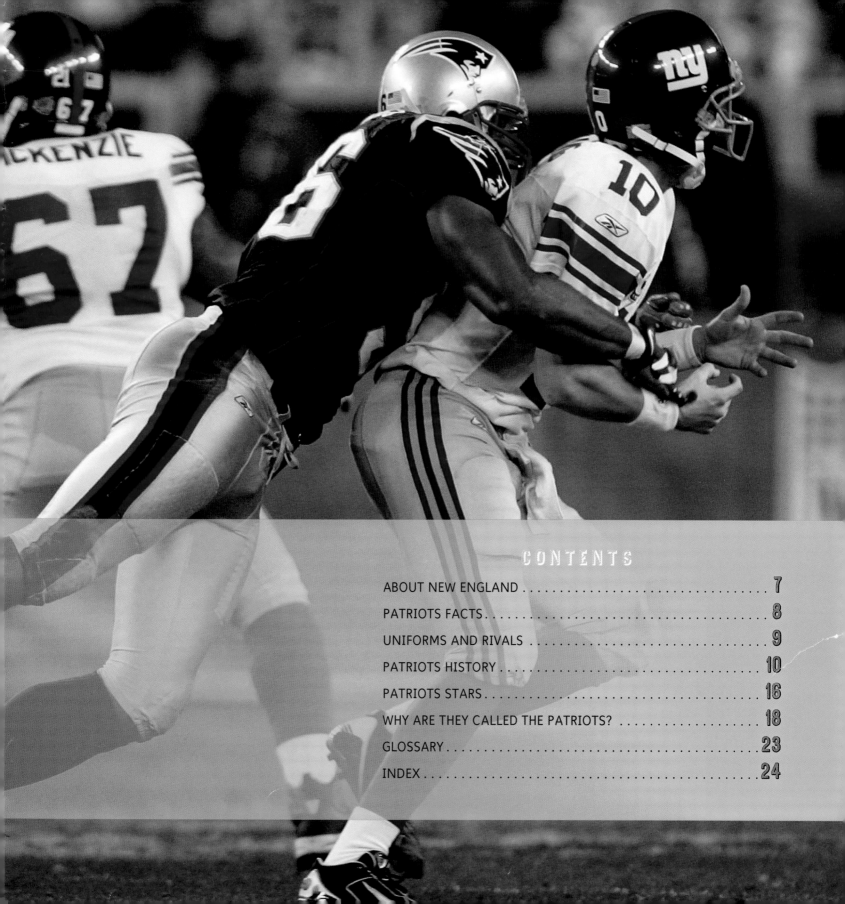

# CONTENTS

SUPER BOWL CHAMPIONS

New England is an area in northeastern America. It is where many people from England sailed to hundreds of years ago. Boston, Massachusetts, is a city in New England. It is near a **stadium** called Gillette Stadium that is the home of a football team called the Patriots.

... BOSTON IS ONE OF THE OLDEST CITIES IN THE UNITED STATES ...

7

## PATRIOTS FACTS

First season:

**1960**

Conference/division:

**American Football Conference, East Division**

Super Bowl championships:

**XXXVI, February 3, 2002 / 20–17 versus St. Louis Rams**
**XXXVIII, February 1, 2004 / 32–29 versus Carolina**
**Panthers**
**XXXIX, February 6, 2005 / 24–21 versus Philadelphia**
**Eagles**

Training camp location:

**Foxborough, Massachusetts**

NFL Web site for kids:

**http://nflrush.com**

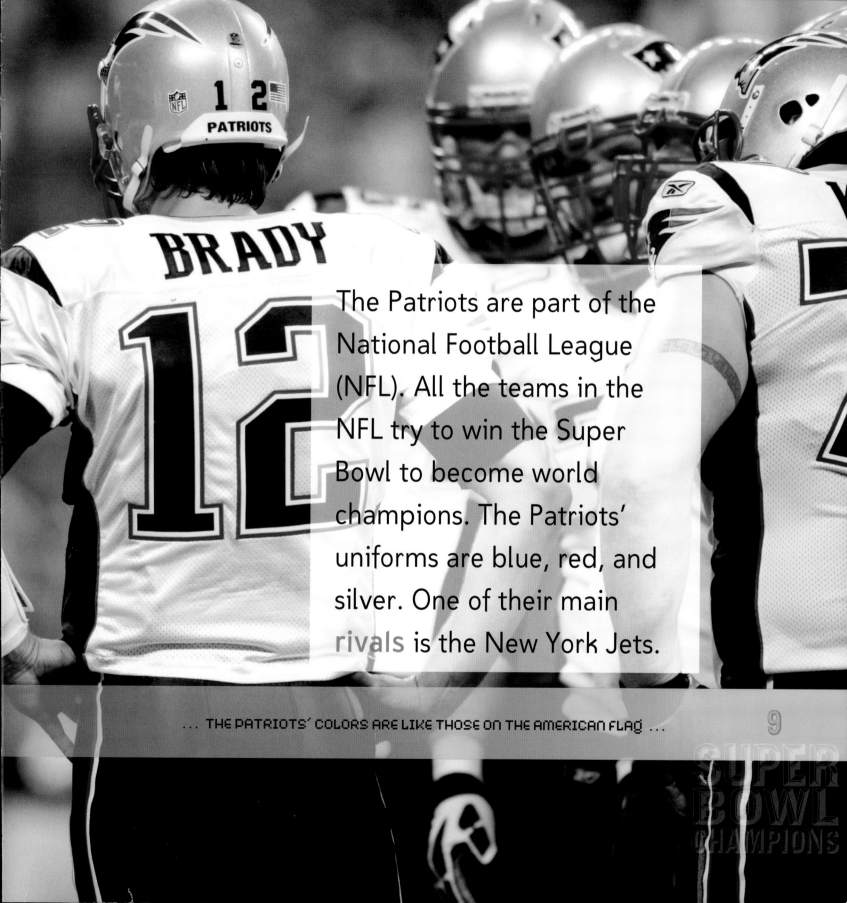

The Patriots are part of the National Football League (NFL). All the teams in the NFL try to win the Super Bowl to become world champions. The Patriots' uniforms are blue, red, and silver. One of their main **rivals** is the New York Jets.

SUPER BOWL CHAMPIONS

The Patriots played their first season in 1960. They were part of a different league called the American Football League (AFL) then. The Patriots almost won the AFL championship after the 1963 season. But in most seasons, they lost a lot of games.

SUPER BOWL CHAMPIONS

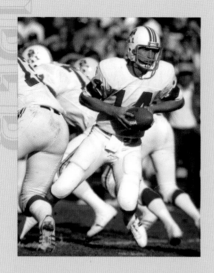

Tough quarterback Steve Grogan led New England to the playoffs after the 1976 and 1978 seasons. The Patriots got to Super Bowl XX (20), but they lost.

... STEVE GROGAN (LEFT) AND TOM BRADY (RIGHT) ...

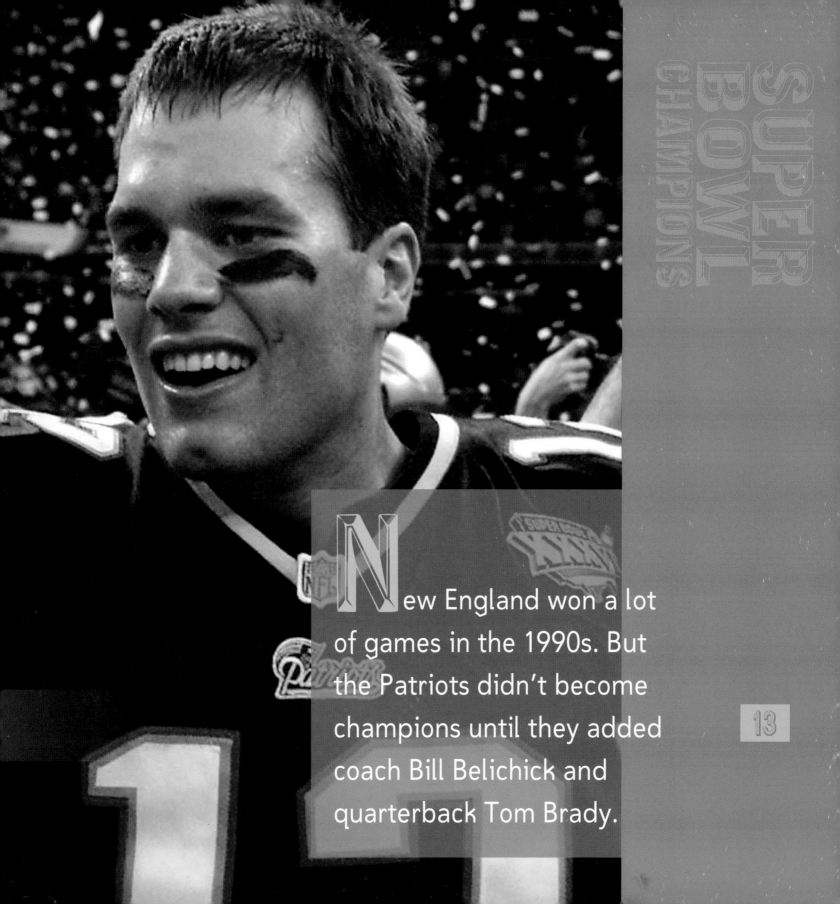

Νew England won a lot of games in the 1990s. But the Patriots didn't become champions until they added coach Bill Belichick and quarterback Tom Brady.

13

SUPER BOWL CHAMPIONS

After the 2001 season, the Patriots won Super Bowl XXXVI (36). They won Super Bowls XXXVIII (38) and XXXIX (39) too! They were almost champions again after the 2007 season. But they lost Super Bowl XLII (42).

Say It Like This

Gino
Cappelletti:

*JEE-noh cap-uh-
LEH-tee*

Two of the Patriots' first stars were Gino Cappelletti and John Hannah. Cappelletti was a wide receiver who also kicked **field goals**. Hannah was a big guard who blocked hard.

... GINO CAPPELLETTI (LEFT) AND JOHN HANNAH (RIGHT) ...

SUPER BOWL CHAMPIONS

17

## WHY ARE THEY CALLED THE PATRIOTS?

America fought a war to be free from England in the 1700s. People who fought for America were called Patriots. There were a lot of Patriots in New England, and many battles took place there.

Say It Like This

Vinatieri:

**vin-uh-tee-AIR-ee**

Stanley Morgan was a speedy receiver in the 1980s. He set a team **record** for touchdown catches. Kicker Adam Vinatieri was another Patriots star. He made many field goals that helped the Patriots win three Super Bowls.

... ADAM VINATIERI WAS A GREAT KICKER, EVEN WHEN PLAYING IN SNOW ...

... JEROD MAYO MADE 98 TACKLES IN HIS FIRST NFL SEASON ...

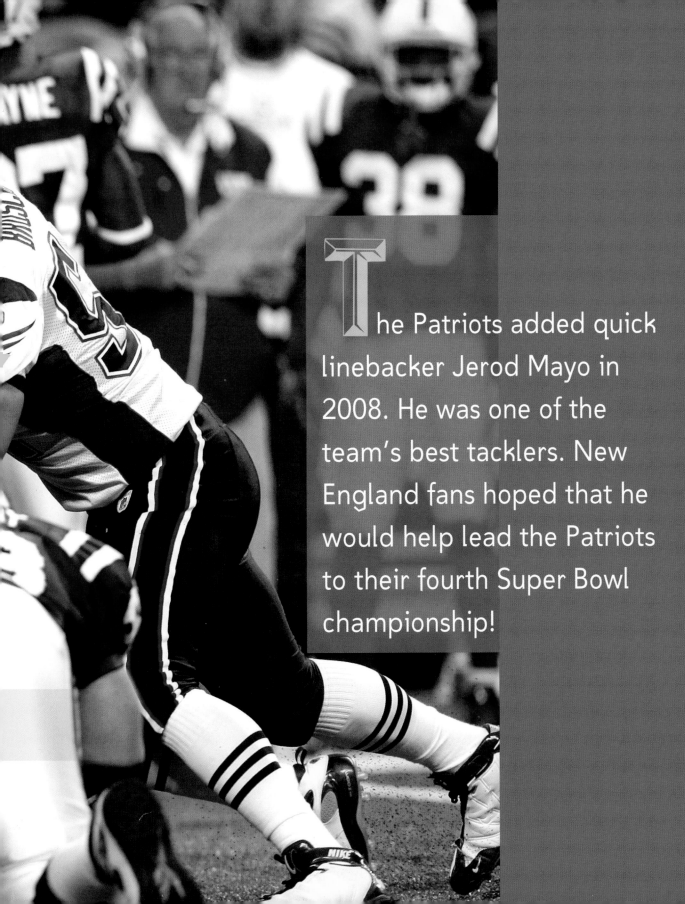

The Patriots added quick linebacker Jerod Mayo in 2008. He was one of the team's best tacklers. New England fans hoped that he would help lead the Patriots to their fourth Super Bowl championship!

21

SUPER BOWL CHAMPIONS

SUPER BOWL CHAMPIONS

# GLOSSARY

field goals — plays where a kicker kicks the ball through the goalposts to score three points

league — a group of teams that all play against each other

playoffs — games that the best teams play after a season to see who the champion will be

record — something that is the best or most ever

rivals — teams that play extra hard against each other

stadium — a large building that has a sports field and many seats for fans

23

# INDEX